Look Mom...
No Cavities

A Book On How To
Raise A Cavity-Free Child!

Gregory F. George, D.D.S.
Second Edition

A Publication Of:

GFG
PRESS, INC.

Look Mom...No Cavities!

Published by GFG Press Inc.
GFG Press, Box 548
PRESS, INC. Buffalo, New York 14231

Copyright © Gregory F. George, D.D.S. 1998, 2001
All Rights Reserved
Editor: Jordana Halpern Geist
Cover Design: HyperDesign, Inc.
Book Design: John D. Valerio, White & Co., Inc.

Second Edition 2001

ISBN #: 0-9662475-3-1

Printed in the U.S.A.

For information on GFG Press Books and other products, including sales inquires and special prices for bulk quantities, write to the address above, or contact GFG Press, Inc. at 1-888-292-1991.

For general information and news updates visit our website at www.lookmom.com

This publication is directed towards parents and young children concerned about dental health. Hopefully, the information contained herein will be useful and help-ful to them. However, it should not be viewed as dental advice and readers should understand that the author and publisher are not rendering professional dental ser-vices to them. Readers should consult their personal dentist about their individual dental health care. The author, publisher and all other persons associated with this publication disclaim any liability arising out of, or relating to, any reliance upon information contained in this publication.

Acknowledgements

A special thanks to everyone who helped me with this book: Thanks to my father, who always encouraged me to reach for the stars and to help other people. Thanks to my mother, who taught me the Golden Rule and that we can do and be anything we really want if we want it enough. Thanks to my stepmother, who taught me about unconditional love and selflessness. My wife and children, who were patient enough to allow me to write this book and whose love on a daily basis fills my life, deserve extra special mention. Finally I wish to thank the wonderful group of people I work with at Pediatric Dental Care, who make every day at work fun, and the thousands of patients, parents and friends in my dental practice, who have taught me so much.

Table of Contents

The Goal:
100% Cavity-Free

*"Raising cavity-free children
can be an attainable, realistic goal for all
parents. All that is required is a little extra
care and use of an easy-to-follow program
that requires less than ten minutes a day."*

The Goal:
100% Cavity-Free

Dear Parents:

Would you like to learn about a simple, effective program that will help you raise cavity-free children? It takes less than ten minutes a day and is easy-to-follow. And it works.

Three years ago, a mother came into my practice with her young children, ages three, five and nine. Although I'm proud to say that the children's experiences were great, it was difficult for their mom, who was very disappointed to learn that there were seven cavities to be filled for the three of them that day.

Her reaction was one of frustration and disappointment. "What can I do to make our next visit better?" she asked. "My kids are brushing, and I don't know what else to do for them."

As I've done for many years with many parents, I immediately reassured her that there was a lot she could do to keep her children's teeth cavity-free and healthy. I gave her tips on brushing techniques, healthy food options, and we discussed preventative treatments that would strengthen tooth enamel.

That evening I went home and started writing this book.

As the father of two young children, I know how important it is to give our children the best possible start in life when it comes to good dental care.

As a pediatric dentist and surgeon for the past twenty years, I have spoken to thousands of concerned parents about how to raise healthy, cavity-free children. But my goal is not simply preventing cavities; I have always tried to promote daily dental hygiene because it is fundamental to total health care.

Parents often ask me if it's really possible to raise cavity-free children. The answer is YES! If you follow the practical advice in this book, your child will never need to experience the painful or frightening sensations that accompany tooth decay. With a little extra care, your toddler will not experience the early loss of front teeth or have to live with large black fillings. Your child will never need to chew on one side of his mouth to avoid pain or be teased about bad breath caused by dental decay. Your child may even avoid having to wear braces that can become necessary when teeth are removed early due to dental decay.

In the first edition of this book, I tried to include as many answers to the questions I hear daily, in a format that would be easy for parents and caregivers of young children to use. Since the book's first printing, I've met many more people who have presented me with a whole new set of important questions to answer. Responding to the needs of people who believe in the importance of good dental hygiene for kids is the way the whole project started, and I think this updated version of the book will better serve your needs in your quest for raising cavity-free children.

The Cavity-Free Plan is an easy-to-follow program that requires less than ten minutes a day.

In the following pages, I'll show you how to teach your child skills and habits that they will carry through their lives and pass on to their own children.

I'll outline many preventative treatments that can strengthen your children's teeth and keep them cavity-free.

I will also discuss the role of food choices and eating habits in cavity formation. Because a child's diet is a major factor in dental health you have a tremendous amount of control when it comes to choosing foods that help prevent tooth decay.

Finally, we'll discuss how establishing a relationship with a caring dentist can enhance your efforts in raising a cavity-free child. If your child's dentist has not yet seen this book, please feel free to highlight any points you may want to share.

The ideas and techniques in this book will work extremely well for most children. Unfortunately, some children's teeth do grow in with structural defects, existing cavities or an inherited genetic trait that makes them more susceptible to decay. Although these children may require additional services, the information in this book will help reduce their odds for developing more cavities.

We can all be players in the effort to gain control of our children's dental well being. You've already taken a positive step by picking up this book. Now I ask you for about an hour of your time. It's a small investment to make in exchange for the healthy smile you'll see on your child's face for many years to come.

Sincerely,

Gregory F. George, D.D.S.

The Benefits Of Cavity Prevention

"From a very early age,
children become conscious of their
appearance. Healthy teeth play an important
role in every child's self-image and self-
confidence levels. A healthy smile immediately
attracts positive attention from neighbors,
teachers, peers and other family members."

The Benefits Of
Cavity Prevention

Flip through a family photo album and take note of what catches your eye. I'm willing to bet that the picture of your family and friends wearing great big smiles is the first thing you see almost every time.

Starting as babies, children learn to pose for the camera, quickly recognizing that a happy smile brings a positive response. A healthy smile plays such an important role in the face we project to the world, and attracts positive attention from family members, neighbors, teachers, and peers.

A child's smile is a window to his or her own personal sense of image and confidence. Children who have clean, bright smiles are more likely to feel comfortable in social settings and speak with fewer inhibitions than children who have black decay marks, bad breath or teeth growing in the wrong direction.

As parents, we want to help our children to be their best, inside and out. Achieving a beautiful smile is a relatively simple accomplishment. With less than ten minutes a day, we can help our children build self-esteem and learn healthy dental habits.

NATURAL TEETH FOR A LIFETIME

Modern advances in dental technology have changed our attitudes about teeth. Many of our parents and grandparents considered losing teeth a normal part of the aging process. Today, most of us can and will keep our teeth for a lifetime.

That kind of progress has brought us many positive benefits. We can maintain healthier, more diverse diets throughout our lives, crunching on apples without ever worrying about denture slippage. We can save time and money avoiding denture fittings and cleanings. And because natural teeth support facial muscles, we can even look younger and ultimately feel younger.

Sometimes parents ask me why it is so important to keep our children's teeth cavity -free. While we have come far with restorative technologies, and the current choices for tooth repairs are varied and growing, it is still much better to avoid getting a cavity in the first place.

Cavities weaken the structure of our natural teeth. Once the decayed part of a tooth is removed, a seam between the filling and tooth will be more prone to future breakdown, making it an easy target for dental problems down the road.

A tooth without a cavity is a lot less trouble than a tooth with a cavity. Fillings today may be quick and easy, but we're still waiting for the perfect filling material to be invented. Some fillings wear faster than real teeth while others expand or shrink. Some are sensitive to hot or cold temperatures and some will fall out as the sealer or glue dissolves away over time. Others crack after excessive, repeated chewing. Often, fillings involve giving your child a local anesthetic such as Novocain, or a relaxing gas such as nitrous oxide, also known as laughing gas. And, even though most fillings today are totally painless, the reality is that your child will never confuse a cavity-filling session with a trip to the amusement park.

Finally, let's not forget the inconvenience caused for children who miss school or extracurricular activities, and for parents who often miss work while their children's teeth are being restored.

In the following chapters I will explain how dental and oral bacteria work, which bacteria are bad, and how we can reduce the amount of bad bacteria. I'll also explain why teeth are attacked by dental decay and how we can minimize the damage caused by bacteria.

I will show you how you can make your children's teeth stronger using easy techniques at home. And I will offer suggestions for treatments, which your dentist can provide, that are proven, sure-fire ways of stopping decay.

There is no reason why your children can't grow up with great looking teeth that function well, enhance good speech development, and help them get optimum nutrition. Let's go on to discuss what we can do to prevent decay and to set the groundwork for maintaining a lifetime of healthy smiles.

BENEFITS OF CAVITY PREVENTION
- Bright, white smile
- Happy, confident child
- Stronger teeth for a lifetime
- No need for invasive procedures such as drilling, fillings, general and local anesthetics
- Save time and money
- Happier visits to the dentist for everyone

The ABC's Of Keeping Teeth Strong

"Most children eat three meals plus three snacks daily. That means that the average child is exposed to acid on their tooth enamel for at least two hours every day."

The ABC's Of Keeping Teeth Strong

Understanding the links between bacteria and carbohydrates and our teeth is an essential component to our cavity prevention program. The better we understand the links, the better we can protect our children from developing cavities right from the start.

The ABC model of the decay triad

I like to use the A, B, C model of tooth decay. This emphasizes the crucial point that cavities result from a combination of three basic elements:

A= A Tooth
B= Bacteria
C= Carbohydrates

A: Teeth

Let's start with teeth, which are made up of three parts: enamel, dentin and pulp. The enamel is the protective outer layer; a white coating that is very strong and dense. Dentin is the middle layer that is not as hard, and more yellow. The pulp is the nerve center and the blood supply of the tooth.

Enamel, the outer layer, is the part of the tooth we can most easily reach and protect. It is also the hardest part of the tooth, so if we do our job in helping enamel stay strong, it can provide daily protection to teeth for a lifetime.

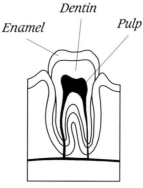

Three parts of the tooth

Bricks And Mortar

To explain the decay process, I like to use a bricks and mortar analogy. Enamel, examined under a microscope, looks something like a brick wall, with mortar holding the

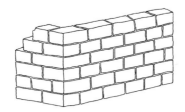

Enamel is a lot like a brick wall

bricks in place. Now, imagine a wall where the mortar starts to dissolve and some of the bricks fall out. This is exactly how a tooth decays. If the pH, a measure of acidity and alkalinity, reaches a high acidic level for a lengthy period of time, some of the mortar begins to dissolve. When too much mortar is lost, bricks start to fall out.

We've all seen solid walls break down, usually due to damaging elements such as weather. Teeth break down in much the same way. When Strep mutans bacteria are fed with foods such as sugar or starch, an acid that dissolves tooth enamel is quickly produced. This dissolving acid may create a hole (see below). Once started, bacteria moves into the hole where it hides from your toothbrush and floss. The bacteria continues to produce more acid and to dissolve more tooth substance, creating decay.

A decayed tooth is like a brick wall with weak mortar and missing bricks

The goal for us as parents then, is to strengthen our children's enamel as much as possible. If we can keep all the bricks, so to speak, in place and not allow the mortar to dissolve, we will keep our children's teeth strong and decay-free.

B: Bacteria

Bacteria are one-celled organisms that are involved in fermentation, putrefaction, infectious diseases, or nitrogen fixation. Many different types of bacteria — some good, some not so good — live in our mouths. One type of not-so-good bacteria is Strep mutans.

These bacteria are located primarily on the outer layer of teeth. When in the presence of a fermentable carbohydrate such as sugar, Strep mutans can cause an acidification of dental plaque. If the acidic levels in the saliva reach a pH level of 5.2 or lower, (7.0 is neutral), tooth enamel can demineralize. The lower the pH, the higher the acidic level - meaning that the potential for enamel to demineralize becomes greater.

If a tooth is assaulted by this bacterial acid for an extended period of time, a hole will develop in the tooth's enamel wall. Bacteria will breed in this hole, eventually dissolving into the next layer of the tooth, forming a cavity.

When given a simple carbohydrate such as candy, bacteria will use the sugar to produce acid. Each exposure to simple carbohydrates results in about twenty minutes of acid production. If our children eat three meals plus three snacks daily, they will be exposed to acid on their tooth enamel for at least two hours every day.

Most of the time, teeth can handle the assault of this acid using natural defenses found in the saliva. An overwhelming presence of bacteria or plaque, however, may overwhelm our natural defenses, leading to decay and cavities.

C: Carbohydrates

Carbohydrates are a necessary food group for our children's healthy growth and development. When it comes to teeth, however, there are good and bad carbohydrates.

So-called simple carbohydrates found in candy, cookies and sweet cereals have a relatively simple biochemical structure. They are quickly and easily broken down (digested) into their component parts (sugars). The process of digestion begins in the mouth as soon as the carbohydrate foods are mixed with saliva making the sugars immediately available to oral bacteria. As mentioned earlier, this will result in acid production that is harmful to teeth.

Complex carbohydrates which are found in grains and vegetables, have a more complicated biochemical structure. These foods take longer to break down as they require acids found in the stomach. Because complex carbohydrates are not significantly digested by the relatively weak action of saliva, the oral bacteria is deprived of the component sugar they need for fuel. Complex carbohydrates result in a much lower production of the enamel dissolving acid in the mouth.

If we can limit the amount of bad carbohydrates we give our children, we will limit the amount of damaging acid production, and thereby keep their teeth as strong as possible.

In Chapter Five, I discuss in greater detail the role that carbohydrates play in cavity prevention or production.

What are cavities and what causes them?

Stated simply, a cavity is tooth decay, generally characterized by yellow, brown or black spots and possibly painful sensations. Cavities form when Strep mutans bacteria consume sugars and starches, producing an acid that dissolves the outside coating of the tooth. If you take away any one of the three essential elements — tooth, bacteria or carbohydrate — you take away the possibility for a cavity. Since we really cannot remove any of these three elements, we must work to control them in preventing decay for our children's teeth.

How can I lower the bacteria and acid levels in my child's mouth?

A vaccine for Strep mutans is being developed, but until it becomes available, you need to decrease the amount of cavity-forming bacteria in your child's mouth. When you alter the bacterial component, you help protect your child's teeth against cavities.

Try to keep your child's teeth as bacteria-free as possible with methods such as brushing, flossing or wiping, discussed in detail in Chapter Four. Brushing and flossing helps remove food from the teeth, but more importantly, it actually decreases the amount of damaging bacteria on the surface of the teeth.

Brushing teeth three times a day is an important habit that keeps the amount and concentrations of bacteria low, so that acid levels are also low. The importance of good oral hygiene is impossible to overstate since it is a major component in keeping bacteria at bay.

When is bacteria most active?

Bacteria is most active while we sleep at night, when our saliva levels are lowest. Also remember that every time our children eat meals or snacks, bacteria is producing acid. Your children are exposed to acid on their tooth enamel for at least two hours every day, and even more if they are constantly snacking throughout the day.

The Dangers Of Tooth Decay

"In many instances, infant cavities
can lead to problems down the road that
are much more easily avoided than fixed."

The Dangers Of
Tooth Decay

Anyone who has had a cavity will understand the pain associated with it. You also know how it feels to have one repaired. For those few and lucky parents who do not know, believe me, you do not want your child to get dental decay.

Treating children with dental problems can often be a challenge. At two- or three-years old, children will not have the verbal skills to tell us if they are feeling pain. They may even believe the pain to be a normal sensation and simply live with it since they don't know any better. Leaving chronic discomfort and decay untreated could lead to many years of dental problems.

In most instances, infant cavities can lead to complications that are much more easily avoided than fixed. If decay reaches the pulp area, then an infection inside the tooth (abscess) will cause pain to your child. This usually results in an unhappy child who is kept awake at night and is fussy during the day because of discomfort and pain. If an abscess occurs in a baby tooth, the permanent tooth may be damaged in the course of the infection, causing it to be misshapen, or marked by unsightly white, yellow or brown spots. An abscessed baby tooth may also cause a permanent tooth to change its normal path of growth.

It's so important to follow a program that stops cavity production before it starts. The few minutes you invest in your child's dental well being each day could reward you and your child with a lifetime of healthy teeth.

My friends are taking their one-year-old children to the dentist, but my mother says she didn't take me until I was three-years-old. What's the right age for a first visit to the dentist?

Generally, a first dental visit should take place around one year of age or upon eruption of the first tooth. I have seen far too many twelve- to eighteen-month-old children who have had to undergo general anesthesia because of early decay that went undetected.

I also think it's great to introduce toddlers to their dentist early on, to help them become comfortable with the idea. If you have an older child who already visits the dentist, bring your infant along. Your younger child can meet the dentist and it's a good opportunity for your dentist to take a first look at your toddler's dental progress.

But doctor, they're just baby teeth. Why should I worry about cavities?

Past generations may have shrugged off concerns about cavities in baby teeth. Well-meaning friends and relatives may have said, "Don't worry about brushing, your baby's teeth will fall out and your little boy or girl will get new teeth soon." Guess what? They gave you bad advice.

Cavity prevention should begin with infants. Picture the tiny teeth of a baby. Those little teeth have roots in the jaw, and inside these roots are nerves and blood vessels which are in turn connected to the brain, the heart and the rest of the body. It stands to reason that we want to avoid a potential connection between a bacterial infection (cavity) and these vital organs.

Even if my toddler does get a cavity in her baby teeth, won't it eventually come out when her adult teeth grow into place?

Yes, that tooth will fall out, but a cavity that occurs in a baby tooth will still need to be cleaned and filled in order to prevent further decay and decrease the possibility of infection. Once the cavity has been filled, the region where the original tooth is restored becomes more prone to future breakdown. If a tooth needs to be removed because of severe decay or infection, it may become necessary for your child to wear a dental appliance to make sure that space is maintained for her permanent tooth.

No matter how gentle and comforting we are, drilling, filling or pulling teeth are all procedures that may be frightening for our young children. We want to avoid these procedures if at all possible.

Can giving my baby a bottle in bed really do her harm? After all, she doesn't have any teeth yet.

Letting a baby go to sleep with a bottle is one of the

prime causes of a special type of decay called *nursing bottle decay* or *baby bottle decay*. It is an extremely destructive condition that deserves special mention.

Infant tooth decay typically arises when baby gums and teeth are not cleaned after bottle or breast feeding. As we discussed in Chapter Two, the sugars found in milk or juice are most active on a baby's teeth while she or he is sleeping. Because saliva, a natural buffer against acid, is less present in the baby's mouth at night, acids are produced in greater amounts, exerting their destructive properties for a longer period of time.

In my career, I have performed surgery on more than a thousand infants who had to undergo general anesthesia for extractions and repairs as a result of bedtime bottles or breast feeding on demand — without their teeth being cleaned afterwards. I have also treated many two- and three-year-old patients who have had all twenty of their teeth destroyed by this type of decay.

You can accomplish so much towards achieving good dental health for your infant with this simple bit of advice: Always clean your baby's gums and teeth with a damp cloth or baby toothbrush after feedings. Baby bottle decay is avoidable and you can easily prevent it from happening to your child.

How do I know if my baby has baby bottle decay?

Initial findings of baby bottle decay may include white lines forming on the teeth, usually along the gum line. Later findings include cavities and infection. If you suspect baby bottle decay, please make an appointment to see your baby's dentist as soon as possible.

How do I take the bottle away from my 11-month-old daughter? She is so attached to it and I'm afraid that if we take it away, none of us will get any sleep at night.

You're going to have to take that bottle away eventually, and the longer you wait, the harder the process will be on all of you. My best advice is to break the habit on a Friday night, rent a couple of good videos and be prepared to lose some sleep over the weekend. It usually only takes a few days to break a toddler habit and you'll be doing her a huge favor in the long run. If, after trying the cold turkey method, you feel you must give her a bottle, then please fill it only with plain water.

What is an abscessed tooth?

If decay progresses into the inner tooth pulp and the infection is left untreated, the inside of the tooth becomes rotten and produces pus which may cause bone in the jaw to dissolve. This condition is called an abscess. It is potentially damaging and in certain circumstances, even life-threatening.

If the bacterial infection in the tooth becomes severe enough, the tooth will become a pus producing factory. This pus has to go somewhere, and the only path out is through the tip of the root to the bone. While this process may at first be painless, it is a dangerous condition. Once the inside of the tooth is rotten and destroyed, pain may no longer be felt since the nerves have also been destroyed.

How do I know if my child has an abscessed tooth?

Symptoms of this condition may include swelling of the cheek, chin, eye region, lip or gum. Antibiotics are generally prescribed to control the swelling, but medication cannot cure the infection. The infection can only be cured by cleaning out the inside of the tooth, usually with a root canal, or by extracting the tooth.

Often, an abscessed tooth cannot be detected just by looking into the mouth. Because of the depth of the infection, x-rays are usually required to make a diagnosis. If the nerves have been damaged, your child may not feel any pain while the infection spreads through the bone. But if your child appears to have any of the symptoms described above, or is complaining of pain while chewing, call your dentist immediately.

Can an abscess cause permanent damage?

Yes. During the infection, the permanent tooth which sits at the root of the baby tooth, may become damaged or develop unsightly white, yellow or brown spotting as well as pitting or odd shaping. Infection can also cause a permanent tooth to grow in a different direction than it would have normally, which may lead to the need for braces or extractions.

EARLY EXTRACTIONS

When a tooth needs to be removed, other complications may arise. In addition to the trauma of extracting a tooth from an infant, toddler or child, we now have to worry about space being maintained in the jaw to accommodate permanent teeth. If a tooth is lost before its natural time, the remaining teeth may drift into the gap, and interfere with natural jaw development and the eruption of permanent teeth.

Early extractions may also result in impacted or non-erupting permanent teeth in the jaw. Once this occurs, braces or surgery may be the only recourse in an effort to reclaim this space and get the permanent teeth to erupt into the mouth.

Gap from extracted tooth

Permanent tooth

Teeth drifting into gap, causing impaction and/or non-eruption of permanent tooth

Permanent tooth

Problems caused by early tooth extraction

PROBLEMS CAUSED BY INFECTION

Poor Nutritional Intake

Cavities and abscesses may also result in poor nutritional intake. Certain foods may be painful for your child to chew, so he may stop eating them. Obviously, if your child stops eating nutritious foods, it could affect his normal growth and development.

As a pediatric dental surgeon, I've noticed the remarkable improvement children make in their eating habits once an infected tooth is restored or extracted.

Unhappy Child

Poor disposition almost always accompanies infections. The child who lives with constant discomfort will certainly feel unhappy and frustrated by chronic pain. Because young children may not always be able to explain their pain, it's important to watch for symptoms of infection, as described earlier.

Fighting Back:
The War Against Bacteria

"We want to stop decay before it begins.
One method is to alter the amounts and
activity of bacteria in our child's mouth."

Fighting Back:
The War Against Bacteria

We don't have to let bacteria win the battle against cavities. We have the means and the methods to stop it before it begins to do damage. Once we consciously alter the amounts and activity of bacteria in our child's mouth, we increase the odds of avoiding cavities altogether.

Removing Bacteria

The first step is to physically remove the bacteria, or plaque - which is a bacterial build-up that creates a sticky home for itself on the tooth. The easiest and most effective way to do this is by brushing and flossing your child's teeth regularly.

Parents should be actively involved in brushing their children's teeth until the ages of eight to ten and in flossing their children's teeth up to the age of ten. It's important to remember that until children reach these ages, they will not be as motivated or dexterous as you, even if they think they can be.

How do you ensure that brushing is a regular part of your child's daily routine? One of the easiest ways is to be a good role model. If your children see you brushing your teeth for a full three minutes, two or three times daily, they may be inclined to follow your example.

However, for many parents, brushing and flossing their children's teeth is a daily test of will, wit and patience. Some children take to brushing instantly, while others fight it three times a day. But with a little creative thinking, you can make brushing and flossing fun.

Ask your dentist and other parents for suggestions. Be prepared to come up with new ideas as your child grows. And remind yourself daily, if necessary, that all your hard work is for a very good cause! (See suggestions at the end of this Chapter.)

At what age should I start brushing my daughter's teeth?

Even before your infant cuts her first tooth, it is time to start fighting off bacteria. Get yourself and your child in the habit of wiping baby teeth and gums with a damp, clean cloth at least three times a day, or after every feeding.

One of the most important times to clean teeth is before nap times and bed times, when saliva production decreases. Saliva is a natural buffer that counters the acids produced by bacteria. If your child goes to sleep without having her teeth cleaned, the acids will be able to do more damage to the enamel over a greater period of time.

At what age is my daughter old enough to brush her teeth by herself?

Just as with any skill, some children will be more ready than others to take on the responsibility of brushing their own teeth. However, I usually recommend that parents continue to brush teeth with their children until they are eight to ten years old. After that, your daughter can take over the job, but do spot checks every week or so. And be sure to ask your hygienist or dentist for a verbal report card on how your daughter is doing, as well as for recommendations about any areas in the mouth that may need improvement or extra attention.

My four-year-old son insists on brushing his teeth himself. Should I fight him for the brush three times a day?

Try reaching a compromise that gives him his independence, but leaves you with the satisfaction of knowing the job was done right. After he brushes, do a final "three minute inspection" with his toothbrush in your hand, using a checklist that can be a fun game for both of you.

Three minutes seems like a long time to brush teeth. Is it really necessary?

Absolutely, if you want to get rid of all the bacteria on your child's teeth and avoid the acid production that can lead to decay. Think of it this way. Your child has twenty teeth, each with three surfaces that need to be cleaned. If you spend two to three seconds brushing each surface, you'll be brushing for about three minutes. It's really very little time out of your day and the benefits are enormous.

REMEMBER, TEETH HAVE
THREE SURFACES THAT NEED BRUSHING:

1. Inside Surface
2. Chewing or Top Surface
3. Outside or Lip Cheek Surface

When brushing the outside surface of teeth, have your child close his mouth almost all the way. This will make it easier for you to stretch the lip and cheek away and thoroughly clean the outside surfaces of the teeth.

Now have your child open wide and brush the chewing surfaces and visually inspect inside the mouth for any food remnants. If you see any white build-up on the tongue, you should try to brush this as well, but don't go too far back or you may cause your child to gag.

Finally, do the inside surfaces of the teeth last, as this is usually the least favorite part for children.

What part of brushing teeth is most effective in cavity prevention?

In brushing your child's teeth, you need to be aware of the area where the gum lies over the tooth. This gum-tooth junction is one to three millimeters deep. It really does require the dexterity of an older youth or an adult, to get the toothbrush bristles into this small area and clean out bacteria that live there.

JAB, JIGGLE AND ROLL

In dental school we're taught the jab, jiggle and roll theme, a technique that effectively cleans the gumline of each tooth and chewing surface.

1. Gently jab the bristles down towards the gum line of the teeth, then jiggle them.

2. Roll the toothbrush in the same direction as the teeth are growing.

3. After following #1 and #2 for all of the teeth, inside and out, you can scrub them horizontally, side to side, or in circles.

Teeth should be brushed a minimum of two times a day, especially after breakfast and before bed. Three times a day is even better.

Try to brush for a full three minutes. Some toothbrushes include built-in recorders that play timed music. You can also keep a tape/CD player in your bathroom and choose your child's favorite music to keep him going.

There are so many toothpastes available. Which is the best at preventing cavities?

Today's market offers an excellent selection of

fluoridated toothpaste. I strongly recommend using a brand that is stamped with the seal of approval from the American Dental Association or the Canadian Dental Association. This identifies that the toothpaste has been clinically studied and that it not only contains fluoride, but the fluoride is properly released onto the tooth. When choosing flavors or colors, find a toothpaste your child enjoys using. My children have always preferred using different toothpastes and you can bet I buy different types to keep them happy and brushing.

OK, I found a toothpaste that my daughter loves. Is it all right for her to use as much as she wants?

No! It's so important for parents to pay attention to the amount of toothpaste children use. Most toothpaste contains fluoride, which strengthens the teeth, but can also be dangerous if too much is ingested.

Only use a pea size or smaller amount of toothpaste and have your child spit out any extra as soon as possible. Most kids love to spit so here's your chance to give them the opportunity three times a day.

Children who ingest too much fluoride on a daily basis are likely to develop a condition called fluorosis. This condition can cause permanent blemishes on teeth that will not fade over time. Fluorosis is discussed in detail in Chapter Six.

My one-year-old son seems more interested in sucking the toothpaste off the toothbrush than letting me brush his teeth. Is it OK to stop using toothpaste?

Absolutely. Children up to the age of three really don't need to use toothpaste at all - it's the brushing, flossing and diet that counts.

Which toothbrush is best?

With the large selection of toothbrushes available, you and your child should have no trouble finding one you both like. Look for two basic features that will help you achieve optimum results.

1. The toothbrush should be the right size for your child's mouth. If the toothbrush head is too large, there will not be room for it to move and scrubbing activity will be less effective. If the toothbrush head is too small, certain areas of the teeth will be missed. I recommend a child-size brush, as do most of the dentists and dental hygienists I know.

2. Look also for a toothbrush with a rounded head that has soft, polished bristles. Cleansing action is primarily achieved through the mechanical action of the brush, water and detergents in the toothpaste. Hard bristles do not clean any better and may in fact, damage gum tissue. Electric toothbrushes are very good and will do a thorough job. But they will also increase your costs, and some can be used only with their own brand of toothpaste and/or replaceable heads.

How often should a toothbrush be replaced?

The general rule of thumb is that if bristles are splaying, spreading out or feeling soft, it's time for a new brush. I recommend replacing toothbrushes every three to six months or even sooner if your child develops an oral infection or strep throat.

HOW TO ENCOURAGE YOUR CHILD TO BRUSH

Letting a child choose his own toothbrush is a great way to keep him involved in his own dental care. There are many child-friendly brushes available, from favorite television or movie characters to toothbrushes with handles that glow-in-the-dark, change color or make noise.

As a pediatric dentist and father of young children, I've learned that if we can make the task fun, we win most of the battles before they begin. Here are some additional ideas:

- Take your children shopping for their own toothbrushes.

- Choose a flavored toothpaste that your child enjoys.

- Play a tape or sing a three-minute brushing song.

- Use a three-minute wind-up toy while brushing.

- Brush in different locations, such as the bathtub or kitchen.

- Keep a toothbrush in more than one bathroom for in-between brushings.

- Make up brushing games that distract reluctant brushers. Get downright silly and make that toothbrush talk, dance and sing its way into your child's mouth.

- Give your child a favorite toy to hold while brushing her teeth.

- Give your child an extra toothbrush and doll to work on while you brush her teeth.

- Encourage siblings to brush together. Often, a younger child will be happy to follow an older brother's or sister's example.

- Ask your dentist or hygienist to speak directly to your children about the importance of brushing. Save the sticker they receive from their dental visit, and post it in the bathroom to use as a reminder.

- Try reverse psychology. Some children will brush forever if they're told not to.

- Use humor whenever possible. It's always easier to brush the teeth of a smiling, giggling child than the clamped down mouth of an angry toddler.

Flossing Teeth

Flossing is an important component to our program, because it enhances our efforts in keeping bacteria off the teeth and gumline, especially in areas between the teeth that are impossible to reach with the toothbrush bristles. In addition, flossing has the proven benefit of preventing dental decay and keeps away gum disease. Recent research shows that flossing may also add more than six years to our lives. So floss more and live longer!

When should I start flossing my child's teeth?

Flossing should start when teeth begin to touch each other and the areas between cannot be reached with a toothbrush. There are many different types of floss available, such as ribbon, tape, flavored and Teflon. I have found that my children enjoy the flavored tape floss over all others.

There are also fun shaped floss holders now available that children enjoy using. Try the different options available until you find the one your child likes best.

How often do I need to floss my son's teeth?

Once begun, flossing should be done every day. As with brushing, flossing will be most effective if done before going to sleep, when the saliva flow decreases. We want to remove as much bacteria from the gumline and teeth surfaces as possible while our natural resistance is lower at night.

At what age can my son floss his teeth by himself?

I recommend that parents continue to help their children floss until age ten. It's a practice that requires greater manual dexterity than brushing. If your child insists on doing it himself, make sure you are watching closely and giving guidance.

I think I should be using dental floss on my daughter's teeth, but she makes such a fuss that I keep giving up. What should I do?

If flossing is a major problem, you can try using a water irrigation device that flushes debris off teeth. Although water irrigation devices are not a total replacement for brushing and flossing, they can be an important aid, especially for children who wear braces. Sometimes your dentist may recommend that you use a special bacterial reducing solution along with the water irrigation device.

HOW TO FLOSS

Tear off a piece of floss about 18″ long. Pinch one end between your left thumb and another finger. Wrap floss around that finger three turns. Now do the same with your right hand and wrap floss until you have a 4″ length between your thumb tips.

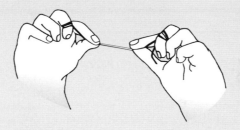

Pass floss between teeth, starting at one side of the mouth and working your way across the top and then the bottom. Slide the floss between two teeth with movement inside and out, until you feel it pass between the contact area of the two teeth. Wrap floss in a C-shape around each tooth and remember you are cleaning two teeth, one at a time, with each pass of floss.

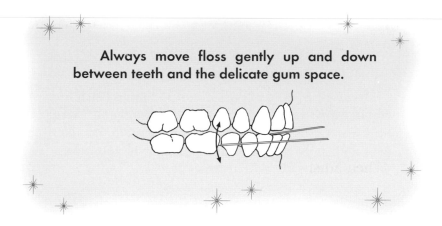

Always move floss gently up and down between teeth and the delicate gum space.

- Remember that flossing only needs to be done when teeth are touching.

- If you find that your floss is shredding, try one of the Teflon flosses.

- You may also choose to try a floss holder. This is a Y-shaped device that keeps the floss tight, instead of using fingers. Many find the floss holder easier to maneuver.

Do my children need to use an anti-bacterial rinse?

Anti-bacterial rinses, available over the counter and by prescription, can be an effective way to lower the amount of bacteria in your child's mouth. However, they should only be used after consulting with your child's dentist, as some rinses can alter taste or stain teeth. Some rinses also contain ethanol, which can be dangerous if ingested. Always check with your dentist before trying an anti-bacterial rinse.

How do I brush my son's teeth now that he has braces?

Cleaning teeth with braces requires extra care, but it is extremely important because braces can trap bacteria and food particles if they're allowed to stay too long on the tooth.

When brushing teeth with braces, think of the mouth as an area with different zones. First, clean the area above the wire, along the gum line. Second, carefully clean the area below the wire. Third, brush on top of the wire in circular motions until the braces are thoroughly clean. Finally, clean the inside tooth surfaces and rough chewing surfaces.

Can dental floss be used with braces?

Although it may take some practice, children with braces need to learn how to floss their teeth, to remove any bacteria or food particles that may be trapped under the wires. It's essential to use a different type of floss, called Super Floss, made of a stiffer material that allows the floss to be threaded through the braces. Once the floss is threaded, flossing is done using the same method as without braces. Our companion video to this book has a great demonstration of how to use Super Floss and how to properly clean teeth and gums for children in braces. If you don't already have our video, please contact us at www.lookmom.com and we'll be happy to send you a copy.

Food: The Good, The Bad & The Ugly

"Some foods actually have a cleansing effect on teeth and are believed to help inhibit decay through an anti-bacterial effect."

Food: The Good, The Bad & The Ugly

As I began to discuss in Chapter Two, food plays a major role in your child's dental health. Fortunately as parents, we can have a tremendous amount of control over what and when our children eat. Teaching our children about the right and wrong types of foods at an early age, can help them develop healthy habits that they'll carry on through their teenage years and into adulthood. As a bonus, we will also be teaching them about good nutrition, as the foods that are healthy for our teeth are also healthy for our bodies.

Feeding Healthy Teeth: Good Food Choices

Foods that are less likely to promote tooth decay include those that are quick dissolving and fibrous, and that don't stay in the mouth long.

These good foods include raw fruits, raw vegetables, pretzels, popcorn and other non-retentive or quickly clearing foods. Some foods, such as milk, cheese and oats, may actually have a cleansing effect on teeth, and may inhibit decay. Please note though, that it is still advisable to maintain good brushing habits after meals, even when these foods are eaten.

Included at the end of this chapter is a sample list of foods that fall into the "Good Foods" category.

Bad Food Choices

As a general rule, any foods that are sticky, processed, highly refined or retentive, are not good for our teeth. Retentive foods include those that stick to teeth or get wedged in between teeth for long periods of time. Sticky foods such as gummy-type candies or processed fruit snacks are also extremely dangerous because they get stuck in areas where they cannot easily be removed with a toothbrush.

In addition to avoiding sticky, gummy-type candies, try to avoid giving your children dried fruits, cookies, snack cakes and other highly processed, refined foods, especially in the middle of the day when brushing teeth may not be possible. Crumbly foods such as potato chips and sweetened cereals that get stuck in grooves or in between teeth, are also more likely to cause cavities.

Included at the end of this chapter is a sample list of foods that fall into the "Bad Foods" category.

Carbohydrates And Teeth

Carbohydrates are an important food group that our children need to grow and to be healthy. There are carbohydrates that are good and bad for our teeth.

Good choices for healthy teeth include complex carbohydrates such as vegetables and grains, which also have the added benefit of nutritional value. Complex carbohydrates break down in the stomach, rather than in the mouth, where they cannot harm teeth.

Among those carbohydrates that are damaging to our children's teeth are sugar and sucrose. It's a good practice to check product labels for simple sugars such as sucrose, refined sugars and corn syrup because they are a major source of food for bacteria. These simple sugars are readily utilized by mouth bacteria and result in increased acid production.

THOSE MENACING GUMMY SNACKS

When I meet parents of new patients, one of the first pieces of advice I offer is to avoid giving all gummy type of candies as well as sticky fruit snacks to their children.

Even though many of these gummy snacks claim to contain fruit juice, they are simple, refined carbohydrates that have extremely destructive properties. Because they are so difficult to remove from teeth, they have become a major cause of cavities for young children.

In my practice I see thousands of children each year who despite good brushing habits, develop cavities as a result of snacking on gummy, fruity snack treats.

Frequency Of Meals And Snacks

It's not just the types of food we eat; it is also the frequency of eating that is important. If your children are snacking all day on raisins, sweet cereal or other simple carbohydrates, the acid levels in their mouths will be high, and they will be more susceptible to dental decay for a longer period of time.

When regular eating times are established during the course of the day, tooth enamel destruction does not become a constant process and the body has the resources to protect itself.

Of course, you can't always deny children snacks and treats. But you can choose to give sweet snacks only after meal times when other refined carbohydrates are already being consumed and teeth are likely to be brushed soon afterwards. In between meals, try offering raw or unprocessed healthy snacks to minimize acid production.

And please remember to use extra caution when brushing and flossing after your children have eaten sticky, retentive foods.

My son doesn't eat much at meal times, but instead likes to snack frequently during the day. I'm afraid that if I cut out his snacks, he won't get all the food he needs.

Children's eating habits can be a constant source of frustration for many parents. And it's true, most kids like to nibble all day long, rather than eat three substantial meals a day. It's important to remember, though, that if your child is eating three meals plus three snacks a day, at least two hours of acid production will result from his oral bacteria. When you add three or four more snack or treat times, you are adding an additional hour or more of acid exposure. And if the snack is a highly refined or retentive type of carbohydrate, this danger zone will be even greater!

Talk to your pediatrician about your child's nutritional needs. Then re-evaluate your child's eating habits and modify them to include more of the good foods, especially during snack time. The earlier you teach your child to snack on carrot sticks instead of sweet cereal, the better his chances are for healthy teeth and a healthy body. And of course, let him have his cookies after dinner when you are available to brush and floss away the sweet crumbs.

What do I do about the cookies and other sweets that are given to my daughter during the day at her day care center?

That's certainly a tough challenge. My dental staff and I have just produced a Dental Health Education Kit, which is being used by one of the largest HMO's in the nation and has been distributed to thousands of students in hundreds of schools in an effort to help caregivers promote healthy dental habits. Try talking to other parents and your school administrator or staff about providing children with healthy food choices. If you'd like to obtain a copy of our kit for your child's school, check out our website at www.lookmom.com or see the back of this book for our mailing address and toll-free number. We'll be very happy to send you a kit.

How do I deal with the snack issue when I'm in the car or traveling with children for long periods of time?

How many of us haven't passed cookies to

outstretched arms in the back seat? Again, it's just a matter of changing your habits and making good food choices. If all you've got in the car are snacks that don't promote cavities such as carrot sticks, celery, pretzels or popcorn, I bet they'll be gobbled up as quickly as less healthy, harmful snacks. If your children are old enough to chew gum, you can offer them sugarless gum. Sorbitol, a sweetener found in certain gums, has been shown to be effective in warding off decay, although in large doses may cause diarrhea.

You should also keep extra toothbrushes and toothpaste in your glove compartment. That way, if your children are likely to fall asleep after stopping for a meal on the road, their teeth will be better protected. And you won't have to wake them up to brush when you reach your destination.

Recently, I've heard about chewing gum that can make teeth stronger. Is this true? Should I give it to my children?

It's true. If your child is old enough to chew gum, there is now a gum on the market that can remineralize teeth, making them stronger. The gum contains a milk - derived ingredient that has been proven to strengthen the tooth's enamel when the gum is chewed for fifteen minutes. Please note that the gum does contain milk derivatives, so it is not appropriate for children who have milk allergies.

I've got teenagers who make their own money and buy their own snacks. How do I monitor their intake of foods that aren't so good for their teeth?

How do we get teenagers to do anything we want? Your best bet is to instill good habits early. Later, give them straightforward information and remind them that having respect for their personal health is a responsibility of growing up. Share portions of this book with them and prevail to their better sense of health and vanity. Most teenagers are very concerned about their appearances, so a healthy smile should be a good reason for them to follow good eating habits.

What do I do at holidays times?

Easter, Christmas, Hanukkah, Kwanzaa, St. Patrick's Day, Valentine's Day, New Year's, Halloween.... Is there a holiday that doesn't include sweets and treats? It's hard enough to monitor ourselves as adults so throwing in the job of keeping candy away from children can sometimes seem an impossible task, especially with so many generous friends and relatives dropping by with gifts. We don't want to deny our children foods, but it's just as important to teach them good habits during the holidays as it is during the rest of the year. Try to reserve sweets for after dinner treats and keep a supply of holiday foods on hand that won't harm teeth. Freshly roasted chestnuts, fruit slices, veggies and dip, or a bowl of assorted nuts to crack can be just as much fun for children as chocolate, jellies and marshmallow treats. And when the feasting is over, let the brushing begin.

A REAL HALLOWEEN TREAT

Here's an idea I've used with my own children at Halloween, to great success. After a fun night of dressing in costumes and trick-or-treating, I offer to buy all their candy and take them to a toy store so that they can choose what ever their candy earnings will buy. The first year I tried this, one of my sons was sold right away, while the other needed to mull it over for a couple of minutes. Now that we've been doing if for a few years, I think they've learned to enjoy selling their candy to me as much as they enjoy getting it from the neighbors.

SNACKS THAT CHILDREN LIKE AND WON'T HURT THEIR TEETH

Fresh Fruits

 Apples, Oranges, Bananas, Peaches, Plums, Nectarines, Strawberries, Blueberries, Raspberries, Grapes, Kiwi, Cantaloupe, Honeydew, Mango, Papaya, Grapefruit, Cherries

Fresh Vegetables

 Baby Carrots, Red & Green Pepper Slices, Celery, Radishes, Cucumber Slices, Raw Turnip Sticks, Fennel Slices, Broccoli and Cauliflower Florets

Lunch Ideas

 Meat Slices, Hard-Boiled Eggs, Yogurt, Hard Cheese, String Cheese, Cheese Cubes

Party Snacks

 Fresh Roasted Chestnuts, Pistachio Nuts, Fruit with Yogurt Dip, Diabetic Soft Drinks and Diabetic Foods, Popcorn, Pickles, Olives

SNACKS THAT ARE HARMFUL TO TEETH AND PROMOTE CAVITY PRODUCTION*

Candy

Gummy Candies, Hard Candies, Fudge, Caramels, Candy Apples, Caramel Popcorn, Lollipops, Peanut Brittle, Candy Bars, Toffee

Snack Foods

Potato Chips, Raisins, Dried Fruits, Sweetened Cereals, Soda Pop

Lunch box items

Fruit Filled Bars, Snack Cakes, Crackers (including graham or soda), Peanut Butter, White Bread

Desserts

Ice Cream, Cookies, Cake, Pie, Popsicles, Gelatin Desserts, Marshmallows

* Please note that the best time to give these foods is at the end of a meal. Your child has already been eating carbohydrates, and of course, you will be more likely to brush the bad carbohydrates off right after the meal.

Sugar Content In Breakfast Cereals
This list gives the sugar content (in grams), of a variety of popular breakfast cereals.

Cereal Product Name	Grams of Sugar in a one-ounce serving
Nutri-grain Corn Cereal	0
Shredded Wheat	0
Puffed Rice	0
Spoon Size Shredded Wheat	0
Cheerios	1
Wheat Chex	2
Rice Chex	2
Nutri-grain Barley Cereal	2
Crispix	3
Concentrate Cereal	3
Rice Krispies	3
Grape Nuts	3
Corn Flakes	3
Product 19	3
Special K	3
Corn Total	3
Smart Start for Women	4
All-Bran Cereal	5
Buc Wheats	5
Toasted Wheat & Raisins	5
Bran Chex	5
Pep Cereal	5
Fortified Oat Flakes	6
Corn Bran	6
100% Natural Cereal	6
Life Cereal	6
40% Bran Flakes	6
Kaboom	6
King Vitamin	6
Cinnamon Life	6
100% Bran	6
Fruit & Fiber w/Apples & Cinnamon	7
Toasted Mini Wheats	7
Bran Buds	7
Country Morning	7
Nature Valley Granola	8
Raisin, Rice & Rye	8
Cinnamon Frosted Mini Wheats	8
Most Cereal	8
CW Post with Raisins	8
Cracklin Bran	8
Honey Nut Crunch Raisin Bran	8
Graham Crackos	9

Sugar Content In Breakfast Cereals (cont'd)

Cereal Product Name	Grams of Sugar in a one-ounce serving
100% Natural Cereal w/Raisins & Dates	9
Post Raisin Bran	9
Country Morning w/Raisins & Dates	9
Cinnamon Toast Crunch	9
Golden Grahams	10
Crispy Wheat & Raisins	10
Honey Nut Cheerios	10
ET	10
Gremlins	10
Wheat Raisin Chex	10
Marshmallow Krispies	10
Raisin Bran	11
Lucky Charms	11
Body Buddies	11
Alpha Bits	11
Cocoa Puffs	11
Honey Comb	11
C-3PO's	11
Cap'n Crunch	12
Cocoa Krispies	12
Trix	12
Pacman	12
Donkey Kong	12
Crispy Oatmeal & Raisin Chex	12
Apple Raisin Crisp	12
Frosted Flakes of Corn	13
Sugar Corn Pops	13
Fruit Loops	13
Cocoa Krispies	13
Frankenberry	13
Frosted Rice	13
Count Chocula	13
Cookie Crisp	13
Donkey Kong Junior	13
Cap'n Crunch's Choco Crunch	13
Raisin Life	13
Cap'n Crunch Crunch Berries	13
Smurf Berry Crunch	13
Fruity Pebbles	13
Cocoa Pebbles	13
Rainbow Brite	14
Apple Jacks	15
Sugar Smacks	15
Honey Smacks	16

Source: Patricia Thonney, Extension Associate Cornell University, Ithaca, NY

Giving Nature A Hand: Techniques To Protect And Strengthen Teeth

"Our goal as parents is to

make the enamel on our children's teeth

as strong as possible, so it can resist acids

that lead to cavity production."

Giving Nature A Hand: Techniques To Protect And Strengthen Teeth

Modern technology has provided us with many valuable tools that enhance our efforts to reduce and eliminate cavities. In this Chapter, I'd like to discuss a number of very successful methods that protect and strengthen young teeth. With minimal cost and effort, helping children avoid getting cavities can be easy and painless.

The Fluoride Connection

Teeth begin growing and continue forming in a child's jawbone from in utero right through to his or her teenage years. This means that even before our child's first tooth erupts, we can begin fortifying enamel and inner tooth layers. It's important to take advantage of this opportunity to strengthen their teeth, because once a tooth erupts, the enamel is fully calcified and stops growing.

One of the best ways we can strengthen enamel on our children's teeth is by giving them fluoride. Studies show that when infants ingest fluoride, their teeth are stronger and more resistant to decay.

Drinking fluoridated water is one of the easiest and most effective ways to ingest fluoride. When fluoride is ingested through drinking water, other beverages or a fluoride supplement, teeth developing in the jaw become stronger and more resistant to decay. For this reason, many communities add fluoride to their drinking water, an effort that has been incredibly successful in cavity reduction. If you don't already know about the fluoride content in your drinking water, call your local water authority to inquire.

If you live in an area where the drinking water is not fluoridated, you should consult with your child's physician or dentist to see whether they recommend a dietary fluoride supplement.

Such supplements are available by prescription and can help developing teeth grow in with a much greater resistance to decay.

Fluoride Treatments

Tooth enamel begins with a very high concentration of fluoride in its outer layers; however, this fluoride can dissolve away over time if it is constantly exposed to acidic pH. The best way to keep enamel from dissolving is to make it more resistant to acid. We can help keep teeth strong by keeping the enamel's fluoride level up to its maximum strength.

The reason you must keep adding fluoride to teeth is similar to the reason you add chlorine to your pool. In a swimming pool, you need to keep up the chlorine level so that bacteria and algae do not contaminate the water. First the pool is shocked with a massive dose of chlorine. Over the season, more chlorine is added in smaller, regular doses to maintain an optimum level. Along with these regular additions, however, it is still necessary to shock the pool occasionally with larger amounts of chlorine, to keep bacteria away.

Teeth are similar. That is why when your child goes to the dentist, it is highly advisable that he receives a topical fluoride treatment. Applied directly to your child's teeth, the fluoride is of a very high concentration. It replenishes the enamel supply, bringing it back to its optimum strength.

In between fluoride treatments, regular use of fluoridated toothpaste and rinses will help the enamel stay resistant to bacteria, acid and decay.

How often should my child receive a topical fluoride treatment?

Your child should receive fluoride treatments from his or her dentist at least two times a year during regular check-ups. Fluoride comes in a variety of child-friendly flavors and can be applied quickly and easily. These treatments, along with other sources of fluoride, will greatly improve your efforts in stopping cavities from forming on the smooth surfaces of your child's teeth.

How can a fluoride treatment at the dentist's office help prevent cavities?

Studies have shown that children who receive regular fluoride treatments can have up to 40% fewer cavities than those who do not. That's an impressive statistic for a procedure that is easy, quick and for most kids, fun.

I've noticed that some toothpaste has fluoride and others do not. Which is better?

I definitely recommend choosing a toothpaste that lists fluoride under its active ingredients. Added topically during regular brushings, the fluoride helps replenish the tooth supply on a daily basis. Your dentist may also suggest the use of a fluoride rinse, fluoride gel or a fluoride varnish that is painted onto teeth to give a long, slow release of fluoride to the enamel.

Please Note: The amount of fluoride your child needs will vary according to her size and age. Before starting a child on a rinse or gel, a dentist should always be consulted. Also remember that your child should spit out all excess toothpaste or rinse containing fluoride, to avoid fluorosis.

Should I use extra toothpaste to make my daughter's teeth stronger?

The answer is no! In fact, using too much toothpaste can be damaging to teeth.

A certain amount of fluoride helps form stronger enamel, but ingesting excessive quantities can result in a condition called fluorosis.

Fluorosis occurs while teeth are still forming in the jaw and primarily affects children from infancy to twelve years of age. Excessive ingestion of fluoride can result in permanent tooth blemishes which are usually brown, yellow or chalky white, giving the tooth a mottled or dirty look that will not fade away.

Swallowing too much toothpaste on a regular basis is the prime cause of fluorosis. Remember – only use a pea-size amount of toothpaste for all children less than six years of age. Since most children are prone to eating more toothpaste than they should, it is very important that you help your children brush their teeth and never allow them to eat toothpaste. Always encourage your children to rinse and spit out excess toothpaste.

How much fluoride is the right amount of fluoride for my child?

It's important to talk to your dentist about the amount of fluoride your child ingests, through every stage of development. Remember in addition to drinking water, most reconstituted beverages are made with fluoridated water. This includes commercially available formula, fruit juices, sodas and even quite a few bottled waters.

Should I give my children fluoridated rinses at home?

Usually, the answer is yes. When used daily, fluoridated rinses can help keep the fluoride on your children's teeth up to optimum levels, providing better protection against bacteria and subsequent decay. Before starting your child on a fluoridated rinse though, please check with your dentist. And remember to encourage your child to spit out any excess after rinsing.

Dental Sealants

Topical fluoride treatments are great for protecting the smooth parts of teeth. The chewing surfaces of the back teeth present a different challenge. Eighty percent of all cavities occur in children's back teeth where grooves and pits on the chewing surfaces trap food and harbor bacteria. These grooves are so narrow that it is often difficult for our toothbrush bristles to properly clean them. As a result, bacteria, sugars and carbohydrates can hide in these grooves, causing decay.

Fortunately, these areas can easily be protected by dental sealants. Sealants are a powerful tool in cavity prevention. They form a barrier between the enamel and bacteria, especially for pits or grooves that cannot easily be cleaned with a toothbrush, floss or rinse. If the bacteria and their acids cannot touch the tooth, a cavity cannot form.

In my office, we've had great success using sealants for children because they are so quickly and painlessly applied. No drilling or Novocain is required. Best of all, sealants have been shown to stop decay on the chewing surfaces of teeth where more than 80% of cavities are formed.

To apply a sealant, the tooth is cleaned and prepared for the liquid resin which is flowed into the grooves and quickly bonded to the tooth.

Once grooves and pits are converted to a smooth surface, bacteria and carbohydrates cannot get in and affect the enamel. Teeth with sealants can also be cleaned more effectively with a toothbrush.

How effective are sealants in cavity prevention?

In studies, sealants have been shown to stop decay on the chewing surfaces of teeth where more than 80% of cavities are formed within two years of placement. They offer a great, painless option when looking for ways to reduce cavities for your child.

How do I know if my child needs sealants?

Your dentist will be able to tell you if your child is a good candidate for dental sealants. In general, children with deep grooves on their back teeth benefit most from this cavity preventing procedure.

How often do sealants need to be applied?

Recent research shows that ten years after they are first applied, 66% of dental sealants are still fully intact. Your dentist will check that sealants are still in place every six months, during regular visits.

What can I do to increase the life of my children's sealants?

Sealants are made of a resinous material that will shrink or expand when exposed to extreme temperatures. To help sealants last longer, children should not chew ice or popsicles and should avoid eating extremely cold or hot foods.

Can all teeth be treated with sealants?

No. Sealants need a rough surface to cling onto, such as the deep, narrow grooves found on posterior teeth. The smooth surfaces of the front teeth can't hold a sealant, but fortunately, they are much easier to reach and clean with a toothbrush.

My son has sealants on all his back teeth. Does this mean he can eat his favorite gummy candies occasionally without me worrying about him developing cavities?

Sorry, but the answer is no. Dental sealants help reduce the incidence of chewing surface cavities. However, we still have to be concerned about smooth surface cavities, where decay occurs on the sides and in between teeth.

Are there different types of sealants available? Which are best?

Some sealants contain fluoride which is slowly released over time. Some sealants are clear while others are white or colored. Your dentist should be able to help you decide which options are best for your child.

HOW SEALANTS PREVENT CAVITIES

Eighty percent of all cavities occur in children's back teeth where grooves and pits on the chewing surfaces trap food and hide bacteria.

Single toothbrush bristle

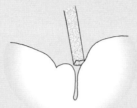

Narrow groove on top surface of tooth

Dental sealants form a barrier between the enamel and bacteria. If the bacteria and their acids cannot touch the tooth, a cavity will not form. Sealants have been shown to stop decay on the chewing surfaces of teeth where more than 80% of cavities are formed. They are an easy, painless way to reduce cavities for your child.

Chewing surface of teeth before sealant is applied

Chewing surface of teeth with sealant applied

Partnership With Your Dentist

By working effectively with your child's dentist and dental hygienist, you can truly eliminate cavities for your child. Every dentist I know would love to see your child stay cavity-free forever and will be happy to work with you to achieve this goal.

New advances in dentistry are constantly being developed. Your dentist is your link to learning more about existing preventative and restoration procedures as well as new techniques. Your dental hygienist can also offer many informative suggestions.

You can also check out our web site at: www.lookmom.com for updates in new advances in preventing dental decay. We change our information as new research is reported. We also add helpful hints from other parents and caregivers. If you have some ideas to share, please e-mail us!

A Practical Plan For
Your Child's Healthy Smile

"Our goal is to keep our children cavity-free
with techniques that will save time
and money. Your child will benefit from a
healthy smile that will make him or her look
and feel good."

A Practical Plan For Your Child's Healthy Smile

In my opening pages I promised that I would provide you with a simple and effective program to help you raise cavity-free children.

As we have seen, it is the enamel — the outer layer — of the tooth that guards against the invasion of harmful bacteria. Strengthening the enamel on our children's teeth as much as possible, along with brushing, flossing, and developing good eating habits, can help resist acids that lead to cavity production. Working together with your child's dentist and taking advantage of the wonderful technologies that are available today will also make a tremendous difference in your efforts to raising a cavity-free child.

The Cavity Busters ABC Method-
Approach for Better Cavity Prevention

The main elements of this program include:

A. Strengthen the tooth's natural physical barriers.

B. Physically remove harmful bacteria and food particles from the teeth and mouth by brushing, flossing and rinsing.

C. Eat foods that do not promote tooth decay.

Develop an ongoing relationship with your child's dentist.

- We must also remember the three factors that are necessary for decay: A tooth, Bacteria, and Carbohydrates. We need to be aware of our ability to limit bad bacteria and bad carbohydrates.

- We need to make brushing and flossing fun, regular parts of our child's day.

- We need to find creative ways to let our children be part of our plan, encouraging them to choose their own appealing toothbrushes and toothpaste.

- We need to guide our children in what and when they eat, ensuring that their diet aids in our efforts to keep acid production down. We need to avoid offering our children sticky and highly processed foods and provide them more raw, natural, fibrous and quick-dissolving foods that will keep their teeth healthy.

- And we need to help make our children's teeth stronger with daily doses of fluoride that are applied topically with fluoridated toothpaste or rinses. Visiting your child's dentist for fluoride treatments and sealants will make it even more difficult for bacteria to begin the decay process.

This program is a lifetime investment. Our goal is to keep children cavity-free with techniques that save time and money. Your child will benefit from a healthy smile that will make him or her look and feel good. You'll feel good too.

I wish you well in raising a cavity-free child. If you would like to see a video tape showing you specific techniques and further discussion of these and other topics, or learn more about our Cavity Busters Kit and Dental Health Education Kit for Teachers and Health Professionals, please contact me by filling out the enclosed order form and sending it to: GFG Press Inc., P.O. Box 548, Buffalo, New York, 14231-0548, or fax the order to (716) 633-2435. You can also call toll-free at 1-888-292-1991 or visit us online on our web site at http://www.lookmom.com.

Sincerely,

Gregory F. George, D.D.S.

Cavity Prevention Check Lists

"Partnerships between children,
parents and dental care providers can help
raise a cavity-free generation."

Cavity Prevention Check Lists

INFANTS
(BIRTH - 24 MONTHS)

THINGS THAT YOUR DENTIST CAN DO:

☑ Visit dentist when first teeth appear for an initial consultation and "look-see." An early first visit will also help your child become familiar with the dental office and equipment and reduce fears that may develop in toddlers.

☑ Fluoride supplements may be prescribed by a dentist.

☑ Oral hygiene instruction may be taught at this visit.

THINGS THAT PARENTS AND CAREGIVERS CAN DO:

✔ Wipe baby gums or teeth with a clean washcloth, gauze pad or toothbrush at least three times a day, after feedings, snacks and always before bedtime.

✔ Avoid putting babies and toddlers to bed with a bottle of milk or juice. If you must use a bedtime bottle, fill it with water only.

✔ Change toothbrush every 3-6 months.

Cavity Prevention Check Lists

CHILDREN
(2 - 6 YEARS)

THINGS THAT YOUR DENTIST CAN DO:

✓ Sealants (a protective coating that covers deep grooves in back teeth) may be recommended.

✓ Fluoride supplements and or treatments may be recommended.

✓ Fluoride varnish, if required.

✓ Complete professional cleaning.

✓ Oral hygiene instruction including flossing technique.

THINGS THAT PARENTS AND CAREGIVERS CAN DO:

☑ Choose a toothbrush that has a rounded head with soft, polished bristles and is the right size for your child's mouth.

☑ Brush teeth 3 times daily, for 3 minutes each time.

☑ Begin using pea-sized (or less) amount of fluoridated toothpaste and encourage children to rinse and spit after brushing.

☑ Begin flossing any teeth that are touching, every night before bedtime.

☑ Change toothbrush every 3-6 months.

☑ Visit the dentist every 6 months.

☑ Be aware of types of foods and frequency of eating.

Cavity Prevention Check Lists

CHILDREN
(6 - 18 YEARS)

THINGS THAT YOUR DENTIST CAN DO:

☑ Sealants for permanent teeth can be provided.

☑ Fluoride supplements and or treatments may be recommended.

☑ Fluoride varnish, if required.

☑ Complete professional cleaning.

☑ Oral hygiene instruction including flossing technique.

THINGS THAT PARENTS AND CAREGIVERS CAN DO:

✔ Begin to transfer responsibility of brushing to child between ages 8-10, depending on child's motor skills and motivation.

✔ Begin to transfer responsibility of flossing to child, no earlier than age 10, as flossing is more difficult than brushing.

✔ Brush teeth 3 times daily if possible.

✔ Change toothbrush every 3-6 months.

✔ Visit the dentist every 6 months.

✔ Be aware of types of foods and frequency of eating.

An easy to follow manual complete with facts, tips and illustrations to help keep your children smiling and cavity-free!

Book

See how pleasant a visit to the dentist can be with this warm, inviting video visit for you and your child to share. This is the video Dr. George gives to each new patient of his, so they can see how cavities start and how to avoid them.

Video

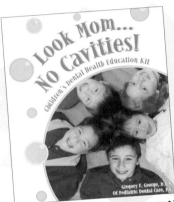

This kit is geared to school nurses, teachers and other health profession- als that educate children on dental health care.

Children's Education Kit

A Total Oral Health Care kit that includes the book, video and the tools one would need for a complete oral health care program.

Cavity Busters Kit

Look Mom...
No Cavities!

TOLL-FREE **1-888-292-1991** (9am - 5pm E.S.T.)

Order a Look Mom...No Cavities! book, video or kits now, and practice this easy-to-follow program in cooperation with your child's dentist.

Mail order form to:
GFG Press, Inc.
P.O. Box 548
Buffalo, NY 14231-0548

Phone: 1-888-292-1991
(TOLL FREE 9am - 5pm E.S.T.)
Fax: (716) 633-2435
www.lookmom.com

Bulk & group discounts available. Please call for details.

A portion of all proceeds to benefit children's charities and dental schools.

☐ **BOOK** _____ #of copies ($12.95 each)

☐ **VIDEO** _____ #of copies ($12.95 each)

☐ **CAVITY BUSTERS KIT** _____ #of copies ($24.95 each)

☐ **DENTAL EDUCATION KIT** _____ #of copies ($39.95 each)

Name: _____

Address: _____

City: _____

State:_____ Zip: _____

Phone:_____

METHOD OF PAYMENT

☐ CHECK   ☐ **MONEY ORDER** (Make payable to: GFG Press, Inc.)
CHARGE TO: ☐ **VISA**   ☐ **MASTERCARD**   ☐ **AMEX**

CARD#: _____ EXP DATE: _____

SIGNATURE: _____

MERCHANDISE TOTAL _____

(Add 8% for NY Residents only) **TAX** _____

SHIPPING & HANDLING $6.95 _____

TOTAL _____

Gregory F. George, D.D.S. grew up on Long Island, New York. He graduated with a Bachelor of Arts degree from the State University of New York College at Potsdam followed by a Doctor of Dental Surgery degree at the School of Dental Medicine at Buffalo, New York. He also completed a two-year residency in Pediatric Dentistry at the Children's Hospital of Buffalo.

Dr. George has a private practice in pediatric dentistry in Williamsville, New York. He has taught at the State University of New York at Buffalo School of Dental Medicine in the Department of Pediatric Dentistry. He is a staff surgeon at the Children's Hospital of Buffalo, Co-Chair of the Dean's Associates at the School of Dental Medicine of Buffalo, Program Chair of the University of Buffalo School of Dental Medicine Alumni Association, and Program Chair of the Buffalo Niagara Dental Meeting. He has been awarded the Pediatric Dental Award through the School of Dental Medicine at Buffalo. He is a member of the American Society of Dentistry for Children, the American Academy of Pediatric Dentists, the American Dental Association, Federation Dentaire Internationale, and the New York State Dental Association, the Erie County Dental Association and the American Academy of Pediatrics.